SELECTED SPEECHES

Gyan Satyagraha
Hampi University
April 15, 2024

Full Faith and Credit
Harvard Law School
March 8, 2024

Gandhi Jayanti
Gandhi Bhavan
October 2, 2023

Democracy's Library
Internet Archive
October 19, 2022

ISBN: 978-1-892628-20-6

Cover art: Cave 26, which is a Buddhist "Chaitya Griha"
or prayer hall in the Ajanta Caves in Maharashtra,
India. Photo by Dey Sandip via Wikipedia.

"Gyan Satyagraha"
Prepared Remarks of Carl Malamud
Kannada University, Hampi
April 15, 2024

Many thanks for your warm welcome, and many thanks to Honourable Vice Chancellor Parashivamurthy, Registrar Thambanda, and Professor Hiremath for inviting me to your beautiful campus. It is an honor and a privilege to sign a Memorandum of Understanding with Kannada University and I look forward to a long future of cooperation.

My friends. Good morning.

I would like to talk to you today about Gyan Satyagraha and why it is an imperative for our times, but first would like to talk a bit about the Servants of Knowledge initiative which I started with my friend and colleague Omshivaprakash who is with me today. We are scanners and we work to make knowledge available for all. This is non-profit and non-commercial work, this is public work.

I've been in the information liberation trade for all of my career. Many years ago, I started coming to India on a regular basis. This year I am making six trips to India.

Why India, you might ask? It is because India is the world's largest democracy, a vast country of a thousand languages, a country with an ancient history and an unparalleled rich culture. If you believe, like I do, that access to knowledge is a human right, India is the only place this dream can begin to become real. You have to come where the action is, and for me that means you have to come to India.

Let me tell you what I do here, what my colleagues in India do here. The Servants of Knowledge initiative got our first home at the Indian Academy of Sciences. We agreed to digitize their materials and also two thousand scientific books from CSRI labs. In return, they let us work out of their basement.

We then added a scanner over in Chennai at the Roja Muthiah library and have scanned thousands of Tamil books. With the help of Bengaluru's own Mohandas Pai, we put a scanner at the World Konkani Centre in Mangaluru and helped them digitize 5,000 Konkani books. We also started manufacturing our scanners here in India, we now have 18 scanners up and running.

We kept on scanning through COVID, but wanted to consolidate our scanners in one place. We approached the Vice Chancellor of the National Law School of India University, and he gave us a nice facility over there so that we could scan the entire law school library. We've now scanned over 30,000 of their books.

For everything we scan, if it's in the public domain, we make it available so anybody can download it or read it online. You can find all those books the Internet Archive at archive.org. If the books we scan are in copyright, we're very careful about them, and make them available to the blind and print disabled and other uses permitted by law, but not for general access like the public domain works. I'll talk more about that in a bit.

After we finished the National Law School library, we were thrilled when Gandhi Bhavan offered us a spacious set of rooms, and that's our new headquarters. They've been really gracious and we love our new home.

Gandhi Bhavan even invited me to give the keynote speech at the Gandhi Jayanti ceremonies, and it was a thrill to be on the same stage with so many freedom fighters and your Chief Minister.

When the Honourable Chief Minister took office, I was very impressed that he told people not to give him flowers but to give him books instead. So I presented him with a USB thumb drive that had 330 books including the Collected Works of Mahatma Gandhi, the Desai Diaries, many Navajivan Trust pamphlets, and much more. He smiled and seemed touched! I was certainly touched, and I was honored to share a stage with him.

We've also been scanning many other things, such as old Kannada books at the BMShri Pratishtana library and community health information from Sochara, a wonderful NGO in Bangalore. We have established partnerships with publishers such as Motilal Banarsidass, Navakarnataka, and the Loka Shikshana Trust.

We've approached many distinguished authors who write in Kannada and obtained permission to scan their books and post them for noncommercial use. We have 50 years of Kasturi Magazine online.

In addition to all the things we're scanning, we've been doing extensive digital harvesting of other open access sites, partly just to make sure they're properly preserved, but also to bring better search engines and tools to bear on these resources to make them easier to use. For all of our materials, we do optical character recognition—OCR— to make the texts searchable, including for all the Indian languages.

Our first big mirror was the government's Digital Library of India system, over five lakh books, a system put together by the Government of India ten years ago that has since crashed. We've also added the West

Bengal Public Library, the Tamil Virtual Academy, the Archeological Survey of India, the Central Secretariat Library, and much more.

Volunteers have contributed other resources, such as tens of thousands of Telugu magazines, thousands of books in Odia, and Arvind Gupta's wonderful collection of children's literature.

Our collection of books has received over 30 crore views. We've also done a systematic harvest of all Official Gazettes from all the states and the Union government, a collection that is updated every day and allows—for the first time—search across the gazettes, including in Indian languages.

You might ask we use Gandhian rhetoric and are based in the Gandhi Bhavan? Our motto is "Scanning is the New Spinning." You know about Gandhi's push for spinning and his iconic use of the charkha. He called that "bread labor," a concept he took from the Bible which said "by the sweat of thy brow, shalt thou earn they bread."

Bread labor for Gandhi meant you should do manual labor every day. In India, cotton farmers and Indigo farmers were forced to send their output to England, where it was spun into finished goods and sold back to people in India.

Gandhi's swadeshi campaign was meant to break that vicious cycle, spinning the cotton locally and turning it into finished goods. It was the first "Make in India" campaign, the goal was no less than purna swaraj.

What many people don't realize though was that Gandhi practiced bread labor in South Africa before he returned to India, but it wasn't spinning cotton. It was typesetting and printing. Gandhiji was a blogger, he was a master of the social media of his day.

Gandhi started gathering news from around the world and adding commentary, and he printed those materials to educate his community and it was through that education that they gained a common purpose and won their satyagraha campaign in South Africa.

At the Phoenix Ashram, everybody's bread labor was typesetting. Even the children were typesetters, it was part of their education. Gandhi was typesetting every day as well. Bapu admitted he wasn't very good at it, he called himself a "dummy" when it came to typesetting, but he did it anyway, because everybody has to participate if they are to raise themselves up as a community. You have to try, everybody has to pitch in.

An educated citizenry is the key to democracy. It was crucial for the liberation of India, but it was also crucial for our civil rights campaign in the United States. Let me tell you a bit about this topic in the U.S. before I turn back to India.

In the U.S., around 1900, we started to get some beautiful public libraries. They were funded by a robber baron named Andrew Carnegie, the richest man in the world, who decided to burnish his legacy by giving money towards the construction of public libraries.

These libraries were temples of knowledge, housed in imposing buildings, built in classical architectural styles. They were beautiful libraries. But, most of them didn't allow blacks or any other people of color in. Carnegie didn't want to offend local feelings among the white elite. The motto of the program was "free for all," but all was not everybody.

In 1902, Carnegie gave money for an amazing municipal library for Atlanta, Georgia. When it was announced, W. E. B. Dubois—the noted scholar and leader of the early civil rights movement—wrote to the library board and said the library should be integrated. The answer he got back was that "Negroes would not be permitted to use the Carnegie Library of Atlanta." They also told him no African Americans would be allowed on the library board.

After a lot of complaining and lobbying and insisting, the library board finally said they'd build a separate library for African Americans. But they took their time, and it wasn't until 1921 that the so-called "coloured library" was built. It was much smaller and far less grand and the budget was tiny. It was a separate library, but it certainly was not equal.

The librarian who was hired was named Annie McPheeters. She started an adult education program there and used her meager salary to buy more books to supplement the far-from-adequate budget provided by the library board. She turned it into a home for the local Black community.

Annie McPheeters told an interesting story about her library. In 1938, a nine-year-old boy who lived two blocks from the library came in and selected two books. He walked up and pushed the books across Annie's desk, showed her his library card, and said he wanted to check them out.

The books were considered "adult books," and the little boy only had a kid's library card, not an adult card. Annie told the boy he should run home and find his father's library card and bring it back, and then she'd let him have those books.

The name of that little boy was Martin Luther King Junior and those two books were about Gandhi. In America, our satyagraha gained inspiration from India.

Atlanta was one of the few cities in the south that had coloured libraries. In most of the South, people of color were not allowed in any library at all.

By 1954, that was still the situation, but then that year the U.S. Supreme Court handed down the Brown versus Board of Education decision that said "separate but equal" wasn't good enough.

The Court's unanimous decision said that education "was the most important function" of government and that the doctrine of separate but equal had no place in our schools or other public facilities. It was a landmark decision.

Of course, even when schools, and buses, and libraries, and playgrounds were "separate" for blacks, they were never equal. Even with that Supreme Court pronouncement—the law of the land laid down by our highest tribunal—there was massive resistance in the South.

Participants in our civil rights movement—our American satyagraha—knew that education was a key underpinning of progress. They started to stage read-ins at libraries. People would go to the library without authorization, pick a book, sit down, and read it. This reading without a license was considered outrageous and revolutionary by the authorities. It was an act of defiance and the authorities were not amused.

In Danville, Virginia, 12 students staged a read-in at the library. They were refused service and thrown out and they sued. A judge ruled that the library must immediately integrate, but Danville decided they'd simply close the library instead.

The same thing happened in other cities. In Albany, Georgia, after a judge declared that the library had to be integrated and open for all, the police padlocked the library to prevent African Americans from gaining entrance.

When they were ordered by a federal judge to remove the padlocks, the library board decided to institute "vertical integration." What that means is they removed all the tables and chairs so blacks and whites couldn't sit together. Everybody had to stand.

In Montgomery, Alabama, where Rosa Parks took her famous bus ride, the atmosphere was tense. It was a tinderbox. Integration sparked a huge amount of activity by the Ku Klux Klan, a lawless gang of racist white thugs. When a judge ordered integration in the Montgomery library, the city again removed the tables and chairs, but a group of very brave young children came to the library anyway, and brought their own tables and chairs with them.

When whites showed up to use the library, the Klan also showed up en masse, taking down names and license plate numbers to intimidate the patrons, as did the police. The white patrons were indeed intimidated and scared off from entering.

In Anniston, Alabama, when the city decided to integrate, two black ministers were chosen to be the first patrons. An angry crowd of racists brutally attacked them with chains, clubs, and knives, sending them to the hospital. A few hours away, that same day in Birmingham, a bomb went off at the Sixteenth Street Baptist Church, killing four little black girls.

The entire south was in flames on that day and the civil rights movement continued their long satyagraha in earnest, demanding their rights as citizens. It was a long fight, culminating in the 1964 Civil Rights Act, but even today that fight continues.

Libraries were in the middle of that satyagraha. Libraries are about education. Not just for children, but for everybody. Libraries are about life-long education, about self-education. They are an essential public utility in a democratic society.

Our civil rights movement in the U.S. realized that, and the same is true here in India. The library movement and the fight for the right to education went hand-in-hand with the liberation of India,

In Baroda, an enlightened Maharaja—His Majesty Sayaji Rao Gaekwad the Third—built a central library which by 1913 had 40,000 books on the shelves and another 25,000 more in storage waiting for a place to put them. Of the 426 large villages, 216 had their own libraries, and there were 140 traveling libraries.

In Andhra, the library movement was the centre of the developing movement for swaraj. By 1920, there were 600 libraries in Andhra. In 1924, The Hindu wrote that "the typical Andhra Library is not a mere storehouse of books but is a centre from which all the healthy activities of the village—social, religious, literary and in some cases political—also proceed."

By 1942, there were over 13,000 village libraries throughout India, with strong efforts in Assam, Bihar, Cochin, Orissa, the Punjab, and many others locations.

In Tamil Nadu, a young man named S.R. Ranganathan sparked a state-wide library movement and he became a leading light world-wide in library science. Ranganthan stressed that libraries are the home for life-long learning. He said that schools should "acquaint students with books," how to read them and use them for the rest of their lives. He called libraries "the primary instruments for universal and self-perpetual education."

Ranganathan is famous for his five laws of library science, laws that are the mantra of every librarian around the world.

The first law is that books are for use, they are not meant to be sequestered and hidden on shelves. The second law is that every reader has his or her book, the third law is that every book has its reader. The fourth is that one must save the time of the reader, that libraries are here to serve us.

Law five—the most important—is that the library is a growing organism. At the Servants of Knowledge, we observe all five laws, but in particular the fifth law. Libraries must grow with the times, they must change and adapt, they must evolve.

Ranganthan, writing in The Hindu in 1929, said that education and learning had deep roots in Indian culture. He pointed to a Kannada inscription found near the village of Wadi from the year 1058, where a sixty-pillared temple had been established, complete with a residential college to educate students on the vedas and the sastras. The inscription noted that there were three vedic teachers, three sastra teachers, and six librarians. With six librarians on staff, it must have clearly been a large library.

The Maharaja of Baroda created more than just libraries, he established schools and scholarships. Indeed, he found a young man named B. R. Ambedkar and sent him first to America to get a Ph.D. at Columbia University, then on to London to get a second Ph.D. and a law degree.

In the U.S., Ambedkar read voraciously, keeping up with the news from India. In 1916, he read in the Bombay Chronicle that the city was going to erect a statue in honor of Pherozeshah Metha. He wrote a letter to the Bombay Municipality saying such a statue would be "very trivial and unbecoming" and that the "fittest and most lasting memorial" would be to build a library instead.

At Columbia, Ambedkar studied under John Dewey, one of the great thinkers of the 20th century. Dewey felt strongly that "a democratic society can only be sustained through education." He had a tremendous influence on Ambedkar and on many others throughout the world.

The depressed classes in most of India not only could not share water facilities and temples with the other castes, they were not allowed in schools. When they were allowed an education, they had to sit on veranda away from the other children.

Ambedkar felt deeply about the right to education. He grew up in a military family, and his father collected many manuscripts and books. When he was a boy, he and his brother had to read texts aloud to the family in the evenings. But, his household was a rarity in the Mahar community.

For Ambedkar, as with Gandhi, liberation came only when the community educated itself about the particulars of their situation. He spoke about how the Raj practiced government "for the people" but not "by the people."

The Raj made the trains run fast, but only so they could expropriate the raw materials of India back to England. They thought this what the people should have, but of course the people themselves were not consulted.

Government "for the people" is not enough for a successful democracy, you must also have government "by the people." Babasaheb wrote that "the continued oppression of the untouchables had to be countered, and at the same time, their awareness had to be built, so that they threw away their apathy and became agitated about the injustice they were suffering."

Under the East India Company, there was a policy of only educating Brahmins. Later, when the Raj adopted a policy of mass education, they did the same as we did in the U.S. Great care was taken not to offend the sensibilities of the upper classes. So, they adopted a policy of separate schools and in many—if not most—cases, those separate schools were never built.

I'm sure you will grant me that education was crucial for raising awareness, to integrate societies and to liberate them in the last century. But why is it relevant in our modern age? We have AI, is that not enough? Who needs to think when there is a tsunami of information on the net?

It is because we as citizens own our government and we have a responsibility to learn and to think if we are to fulfill our ownership responsibilities. We cannot succumb to that tsunami. Gandhi taught us that if all we ingest are trivial things, "all our thoughts shall be tinged with triviality. Our very intellect shall be macadamized."

I put it to you that today, all too often all we have government for the people, not government by the people. We have what my friend Tim O'Reilly calls vending machine government. Citizens deposit their taxes in the slot, and out pops their government.

Efficient government is not enough, we must have participatory democracy. Ambedkar said that "any people, however patient, will sooner or later demand a government that will be more than a mere engine of efficiency."

Despite the flood of disinformation we see on Telegram, Facebook, WhatsApp, and Twitter we do not have the knowledge we need. Today knowledge has become colonized.

For years, I've been giving lectures around India at law schools, IIT campuses, regional colleges. I always ask people if they have access to the information they need to finish their education and do their research.

The answer is always a loud no. Scientific and scholarly information has been sequestered behind pay walls. When I ask students, professors, and even vice chancellors in scientific institutions how many of them use SciHub to find information, every hand goes up.

Public knowledge has become private property, property that is hidden and then mined to maximize rents. To sequester knowledge, to prevent others from accessing knowledge, this is a sacrilege, a sin.

Those who purport to own knowledge bandy about the word "copyright" as if it is some talisman that justifies their actions. But those who invoke copyright to justify absolute control do not understand the true meaning of the word.

Copyright is often referred to as "intellectual property" but that is an awful term, it is not accurate. Even if it is property, as Gandhi teaches us, if one accumulates great wealth one only holds it in trust for the people. The same goes for knowledge. Copyright is not property, it is a trusteeship for the benefit of society.

Some misguided souls have come to view copyright as a binary proposition. They think a copyright registration means they may tell people what they may do with a book or a journal article and under what circumstances.

These copyright maximalists say they have the right to set the price for any and all uses and they must be asked permission in each and every case. This is wrong, it is not how the law works.

The very purpose of copyright is the increase and diffusion of knowledge. Authors are given a limited set of rights for a limited period of time, but the public is also granted a set of rights. The balancing of those rights is the very essence of copyright.

The copyright act of India is a wonderful example of post-colonial legislation. While things such as the Penal Code were inherited from the Raj, the Copyright Act of India was crafted by the new government with the intent of making knowledge flourish in India. Read the legislative history of the act and you'll see the deep roots going back to the Constituent Assembly debates over the Constitution of India.

If you read the Copyright Act, you will see that in addition to the limited rights granted to authors, there are a number of exceptions. This is known as "fair dealing."

Libraries have rights, for example the right to make copies of books to archive and preserve them. They do not need to seek permission permission from the publishers, that right is granted to them under the law.

If you are blind, copyright does not apply at all. Use by the visually impaired is an absolute exception to copyright, and it is codified in international treaties and national laws. I can give you a copy of any book if you are print disabled.

Likewise, if in the course of your research you need a book, I can make a copy of that book for you regardless of copyright. Research uses are an exception to copyright. That is the law and it is enshrined in Section 52 of the Copyright Act of India.

As we learned in the Delhi University Case, if students are furnished materials such as course packs in the course of instruction, copyright also does not apply. This was the pronouncement of the Honourable

High Court of Delhi when it affirmed the right of students to pursue their education.

Copyright is not a binary thing. It is a balance, a balance where the rights of society tip the scales in favor of the public.

Despite that, knowledge has become sequestered. It has become a tool of commerce, a tool of diplomatic gamesmanship.

Some of you may be familiar with the PL 480 program. It was a U.S. law passed in 1954. PL stands for "Public Law," and it inaugurated the so-called "food for peace" diplomatic effort during the cold war. That was where the U.S. Government sold India subsidized wheat. Not only was it sold cheaply, India was able to pay in rupees instead of dollars.

Based on that, the U.S. sent you wheat. It turns out that mixed in with that wheat was "congress grass," which is parthenium and is a toxic invasive species. So the U.S. also sent many of you asthma along with the wheat, but that's another story.

When the U.S. sold India wheat, it found itself sitting on a large pile of rupees. What did the U.S. decide to do with that money? It started buying a huge number of books from India. Among other things, the U.S. bought 25 copies of every single government of India work.

Since government works had limited print runs, that meant that U.S. libraries have the ultimate collection of India books, especially works of government. In 1965, the PL 480 program bought 633,495 books from India.

The other thing the U.S. did—and the U.S. wasn't alone, Russia also played this game—was that it sent subsidized books over to India. This was the so-called "war of the minds." A huge number of old and out-of-date textbooks—over 1,000 different titles—were made available at greatly subsidized rates and sold throughout India.

What did that do? It was a huge blow to the Indian publishing industry. If an Indian author wanted to make a new textbook on a subject, there was no way the Indian publishers could compete with the rock-bottom subsidized prices that the old U.S. books were being sold for.

Knowledge became a tool of commerce and international games instead of the bedrock of education, of self-empowerment, of science, of democracy.

In today's world, with so much knowledge being treated as property, we have to be aggressive if we wish to change that. Knowledge is the key to democracy, and it is the key to the future. Indian students, indeed the people of India who are all life-long learners, should be able enjoy universal access to knowledge.

Satyagraha is the process of methodically and with purpose fighting for something. It is the method for confronting authority, and it the method that we practice in the Servants of Knowledge.

Let me give you an example, and that is works published by the Indian government. The Government of India is the largest publisher in India. There are over 400 publishing agencies in the public sector, some 200 of those are under the auspices of the central government. The Government of India publishes vast numbers of books. For example the National Book Trust has sold over 30 million books, all of them heavily subsidized.

The purpose of this publication is not profit, the purpose is dissemination of useful information, but despite that the government often imposes charges and terms of use that prevent the increase and diffusion of that knowledge.

An example is the Bureau of Indian Standards. There are 19,000 Indian Standards. They specify the building code of India, the electrical code of India, but much more.

Indian standards specify how motorcycle helmets are to be made safe. Indeed, one cannot sell a motorcycle helmet in India if it is not certified by the Bureau as conforming to the standard.

Another standard specifies a code of best practice for entering sewer systems. It explains what you must tell people so they may enter those systems safely. As you know if you read the papers, people are frequently being sent into the sewers and perishing. This standard is meant to protect them.

Indian standards specify the safety of textile machines and agriculture equipment. They specify toy safety and playground safety. They specify how and where fire exits must be provided in schools and hospitals.

Despite that, the Bureau only made the standards available for fees, imposed very strict copyright restrictions, encrypted the documents so you couldn't easily access them or print them.

This policy applied not only to citizens, but to government employees in the state and union governments. Government agencies were required to purchase the standards from the Bureau in order to carry out their statutory duties of ensuring the public safety.

I heard about a meeting of 30 different government agencies who gathered to discuss disaster management procedures. One of the babus stood up and said he though every attendee at that meeting should have a copy of the Building Code of India. The Bureau stood up and explained that they accepted various forms of payment and would be happy to take their money.

I considered these Indian Standards crucial to public safety in India. They are produced using an elaborate law-making process, they are noticed in the Official Gazettes, and they are extensively used in legislation and regulations.

So, in 2012, I started purchasing Indian standards. In fact, I purchased all of them and posted them for free download. When the Bureau objected, I filed a PIL in the Delhi High Court and was joined as co-petitioners by Sushant Sinha and Srinivas Kodali.

We kept the standards online and millions of downloads kept on happening, and we started seeing government agencies posting the standards we had made available on their web sites.

I'm pleased to report that last year, the Bureau folded their cards and now have over 14,000 Indian standards available for free download and we've withdrawn our suit. Jai Gyan.

We've had similar wins in the U.S., where after 10 years of fierce litigation we won decisive victories in the U.S. Supreme Court and in the Courts of Appeal, establishing clearly that the law belongs to the people and that it is fair use for public safety standards to be freely disseminated.

Just recently, in Europe, a unanimous constitutional bench of the European Union Court of Justice—the Supreme Court of Europe—ruled in our favor that harmonised standards for public safety are part and parcel of EU law and therefore must be made available.

The Bureau is not the only government agency in India posting useful information. We've got hundreds of books from the Publications Division which we've scanned and made available.

When the Publications Division sent us a letter demanding that the materials be removed, we sent them a polite letter in response. We pointed out that our use was noncommercial with the intent of making these materials available to the people of India and we quoted the Constitution of India as our justification.

We also pointed out that the government did not have any digital copies of their publications available and offered to send them a copy they could post. And, finally, we respectfully declined to remove the publications from the Internet. We didn't hear back from them.

A similar cycle has happened with numerous other agencies. Each time, we offer to help, we explain our purpose and motivations, and politely decline to comply with their requests.

Knowledge is the key to change, and we can only have knowledge with education. Education is the foundation of a democracy. Only when the people educate themselves will change occur.

If our government does not believe climate change is real, we must educate ourselves and stand up and demand that it do something.

If we believe that growing economic inequality has reached catastrophic proportions, only the people can change that situation.

We own our democracy, but we can only properly be the trustees of our government if we educate ourselves.

If we believe that all citizens must have "equality of status and opportunity"—as it so clearly and eloquently says in the Preamble to the Constitution of India— those are empty words if the means to achieve that are unavailable.

If we believe all citizens must be able to practice the profession of their choice as guaranteed in Article 19 of the Constitution , how can people do that if they do not have the means to educate themselves about the profession they wish to practice?

If we are to have "liberty of thought, expression, belief, faith and worship," where in the Preamble does it say those rights are conditional upon possession of a Gold American Express Card?

Everybody has heard schoolchildren recite Gitanjali 35, Tagore's eloquent cry of "let my country awake." But, look at those words carefully.

That poem is about a world where "knowledge is free." It is about one where "words come out from the depth of truth." Tagore was speaking about access to knowledge. He spoke of "a country where the mind is led forward into ever-widening thought and action."

If we believe disinformation is a pandemic spread by the Internet, the only cure is better information. If we believe government is currently the tool of corporate insiders, all we can do is educate ourselves. Only then can we seize the reigns of power.

Walls around knowledge are the tools of oppression. Access to knowledge is a human right.

We must fight. As Martin Luther King said, "change does not come rolling in on the wheels of inevitability, it comes only with continuous struggle."

In the information age, Gyan Satyagraha will help light up that crooked path that stands between us and that shining city on the hill. Every generation faces unique challenges it must overcome. Gyan satyagraha is the challenge for our time and access to knowledge is our duty to future generations.

Jai Gyan. Jai Hind.

Thank you.

Good afternoon. I'd like to tell you a story today about full faith and credit.

In 2013, I purchased a complete set of the laws of the State of Georgia—the Official Code of Georgia Annotated—for $1,107.09. I scanned the 48 volumes and posted them on the net, and put a copy of those scans on a George Washington USB drive and sent it to the Speaker of the House of Georgia.

The Speaker was not amused.

He fired back an angry cease and desist letter, insisting that the offending materials were the sole and exclusive property of the State of Georgia, which had granted exclusive resale rights to the Lexis Corporation, and that we should heretofore remove said materials forthwith from the Internet, or face unspecified but certainly dire consequences.

We respectfully declined to comply, explaining our radical position that the law belongs to the people, and then sent further copies of the code out to legal aid groups, public defenders, mayors, and libraries throughout Georgia.

More more letters flew back and forth, and on July 21, 2015 the State of Georgia served papers on my person, alleging in the complaint a practice of "terrorism" by me as evidenced by my wanton and flagrant practice of unlicensed promulgation.

The State asserted ownership over 22 categories of Official Annotations, ranging from section titles to Code Commission Guidance to history logs to Attorney General opinions to summaries of judicial cases, all of which they said were subject to copyright, all rights reserved in the name of the State of Georgia.

We lost very quickly in the district court. I basically pleaded no contest. I did the deed. Judge Story said there was no excuse for this behavior, and he slapped a federal injunction on me, ordering me to remove all evidence of the law of Georgia over which I had control from the Internet.

We appealed to the Court of Appeals for the 11th Circuit, where we were joined by the ACLU in oral argument, and we won. Georgia filed for *certiorari* in the U.S. Supreme Court, and we did something that usually isn't done by the winner in the court below: we urged the court to take the case.

The Supreme Court accepted our case and we prevailed. The court agreed with our position that these were edicts of government, which are the law and legal materials issued in the name of the state. Under a 200-year old common law doctrine, edicts of government are not eligible for copyright protection.

The government edicts doctrine precedes and supersedes the powers of the Congress to grant copyright under Article 1, Section 8, and that is because edicts of government are fundamental to our democracy. Promulgation of the law is a fundamental tenet of the rule of law, promulgation of the law is integral to free speech, to commerce among the states, to due process, and to access to justice. In the United States, the law belongs to the people.

We won in Georgia, but I still cannot get an up-to-date copy of the Official Code of Georgia Annotated. Chief Justice Roberts, writing for the majority, said I didn't have to settle for "economy class" access to the law and gave me an upgrade to first class, but apparently the Lexis Corporation does not recognize the Supreme Court's frequent flier program.

The OCGA is only available on the Lexis Corporation site, where they offer "law as a service," law that is subject to strict terms of use, a substantial rental fee, and technical measures that prohibit downloading and repurposing. It is read-only law. It's like a Netflix movie, which you can view on a properly registered viewer if you have been authorized and authenticated, but guess what, don't blink twice as your movie may soon disappear.

Georgia is not the only state that still asserts copyright in the name of the state over edicts of government. Mississippi is adamant that not only the annotated code but the black letter law—the statutes— are their private property, as are all state regulations. Idaho, Tennessee, Arkansas, and New Mexico all assert copyright over their codes. The U.S. Copyright Office liberally grants new registrations over these public properties, despite the Supreme Court ruling.

The same situation applies for jury instructions, written mainly by judges in the course of their official duties, copyrighted in the same of the state, and then given to Lexis or West for their exclusive sales. When you see "Copyright, Supreme Court of Kansas," or "Copyright, Unified Court System of New York," that is a theoretically impossible phrase under the government edicts doctrine, but there you go, the "keep off the grass sign" is impossible to miss.

What can we do about this situation? I believe the answer is staring us right in the face, and it is contained in the Full Faith and Credit clause of the U.S. Constitution. That clause has two sentences:

> *Full Faith and Credit shall be given in each State to the public Acts, Records, and judicial Proceedings of every other State.*

The second sentence reads:

> *And the Congress may by general Laws prescribe the Manner in which such Acts, Records and Proceedings shall be proved, and the Effect thereof.*

Let's look at those two sentences. The first is a self-executing clause. It was meant to handle cases such as debts, where a state court ruled that a debt was valid and must be paid, but the debtor fled to another state with different laws. It also applies to matrimonial issues, contracts, and other nuts-and-bolts issues that present themselves in the state courts. More recently, the issue has arisen in the context of the so-called Defense of Marriage Act.

What does "Full Faith and Credit" mean? As with many important constitutional concepts, the meaning was and is still vague and ambiguous. When James Madison pulled this clause out of the Articles of Confederation, the term "Full Faith and Credit" was an evidentiary standard, but Madison conceded in the Federalist Papers that the meaning was "extremely indeterminate."

Finding the law in those days was difficult. Professor Sachs, in his excellent history of the clause, explains how difficult it was for many years after the founding to get accurate copies of even federal laws. You could get an authenticated copy from the Department of State, but for state decisions, they were often copied by hand, subject to mistakes, and difficult to find and authenticate. Justice Joseph Story complained bitterly about the "loose and irregular" condition of legal materials.

There is still debate about the basic meaning of the term "Full Faith and Credit" in the first sentence, but it is clear that Congress is empowered in the second sentence to impose additional requirements. The first sentence is a baseline, but the second sentence is what Professor Tribe described as a "one-way-ratchet" in a letter to Senator Edward Kennedy in regards to DOMA. You can't weaken the first sentence, but you can strengthen it with the powers granted in the second.

For me, that second sentence is all about promulgation of the law, and I believe the answer is a Full Faith and Credit Act. The act would specify that any edict of government issued by the states and local jurisdictions are subject to mandatory deposit with the Government Publishing Office. A state and local government can pass any law it deems appropriate, and the appropriateness is of course a matter for the courts. But, if an edict is issued, it must be sent to the GPO.

The GPO already does an amazingly good job in this respect with federal materials: laws and bills, the Congressional Record, the Federal Register, the Code of Federal Regulations, the U.S. Code, congressional hearings and reports, the Statutes at Large, and much more.

Under the Full Faith and Credit Act the responsibility of the Government Publishing Office would be expanded to include all edicts of government. State court dockets, the federal PACER system, jury instructions, building codes, state laws, hearings, regulations, attorney general opinions, municipal codes. Everything. The works.

GPO would be mandated to provide bulk access with a clueful Application Programming Interface, metadata in JSON and XML formats, all digitally signed with the GPO seal of approval.

I am convinced that James Madison would endorse this proposition. And, I'm also sure any literalist would have to agree that the Constitution clearly gives the Congress this power, indeed compels it to act, for without taking these steps, the first sentence is but an unfulfilled mandate.

If we believe that Congress may regulate commerce among the states, making the laws of those states available is crucial, for the law is the rulebook that governs commerce. If we believe in the rule of law, we should heed the words of Lord Thomas Bingham in his excellent book on the subject when he says promulgation is the essential ingredient of the rule of law. There can be no rule of law if the law itself is not available.

If ignorance of the law is no excuse, how can we have access to justice and due process if the law is locked behind a pay wall and subject to onerous and arbitrary terms of use by private parties? In a democracy, we must have the right not only to read the law but to speak the law, to communicate our rights and obligations to our fellow citizens.

This is about access to justice, but it is also about innovation in our legal system. In 1876, because state court opinions were not subject to copyright, John B. West was able to create the National Reporter System. He was the face of innovation for the practice of law. He didn't need a license to create this magnificent legal edifice then, but today he would.

Under the Full Faith and Credit Act, the legal services industry will see the full flowering of innovation. This step will not only be good for democracy, it will be good for business.

Today, exclusive rights to our legal materials have been granted to private players, each of which hides the law in private silos. The natural resource that is our legal system, the raw materials of our democracy, have been fenced off and privatized.

In his 1944 Cardozo lecture, Justice Robert H. Jackson said that "the Full Faith and Credit Clause is the foundation of any hope we may have for a truly national system of justice, based on the preservation but better integration of the local jurisdictions we have."

It is time, at long last, to fully implement the Full Faith and Credit Clause. It is time to nationalize the law, to make this public resource truly public. This, I put to you, this is the future of open access to the law.

Thank you.

Prepared Remarks of Carl Malamud
Gandhi Jayanti, October 2, 2023
Gandhi Bhavana, Bengaluru, India

Honourable Law and Parliamentary Affairs Minister.

Distinguished Freedom Fighters.

Dr. Krishna.

Mr. Vishikumar.

Distinguished guests.

My friends.

Good afternoon.

Thank you for inviting me. I am delighted to be here to celebrate Gandhi Jayanti with you today.

I must confess that while this is truly an honor, it has had me scared to death trying to figure out what I might say to you. I've been worrying about this for weeks.

All of you here today have grown up with Gandhi–ji. You have known him and loved him all your life. What can an American tell you about somebody who is an essential part of your national fabric?

However, here we are, so let me try and give you my thoughts on the subject. Please bear with me.

For me, when I think of Gandhi-ji, I think first of South Africa, of the satyagraha there, and how that came to be.

It was in South Africa that Gandhi-ji learned to lead. He reached out to people by sharing knowledge, giving people the means to educate themselves, to become aware of their situation, and of their rights as human beings. Gandhi-ji used knowledge to awaken his people.

His great triumph there was his writing, his re-transmission of news reports, his analysis of the news, his opinions about the implications of the news, and ultimately his creation of communities that understood their rights and obligations under the law, communities to which he taught the nuts and bolts about how to effect change, how to question authority.

Today, some might say he was a blogger. But, one with purpose. He certainly would have embraced the Internet, but of course he would have had very strong opinions about the net. There is no doubt in my mind about that.

You can read his prolific output during those days in the Collected Works or in Indian Opinion. He was a fount of information. With knowledge came courage, and with courage came freedom. Not absolute freedom of course, the fight continued—and continues to this day—but this was his start.

Gandhi's insight that knowledge leads to freedom was not new. Just look right here in Karnataka at the work of Lord Basavanna and the Sharana movement—a movement that created the great Anubhava Mantapa parliament, a movement based on equality and education, a movement that created the great flowering of the Vachanas, a movement whose spirit lives on today, despite its brutal suppression.

The fight for freedom and justice is not a battle that can be won or lost in a moment, it requires our unflagging attention. As Martin Luther King said, "change does not come rolling in on the wheels of inevitability, it comes only with continuous struggle."

Gandhi-ji embraced two very simple concepts in his work, two powerful tools at the core of his practice. The first was the idea of public work.

Public work is work that benefits your community, work done without recompense, an essential part of our function and our duty as citizens.

The second concept that Gandhi-ji embraced was that of bread labor, an idea that he got from the Bible, which teaches "that by the sweat of your brow shalt thou eat thy bread."

This means you must do some form of real labor every day, you must work for your bread. We must respect all work, and especially respect all those who work.

This teaching from the Bible is remarkably similar to the message of the Vachanas that "work is worship." Worshipping is not enough, one must work as the means of showing devotion. As is said today, God only helps those who help themselves.

You probably think of the charkha when you think of bread labor. The iconic image of Gandhi-ji at his spinning wheel, his every day labor. The spinning wheel broke the chain, the chain of indigo and cotton farmers who sent their goods to Manchester, where it became the cloth that was sold back to them.

This was a vicious circle. To grow the indigo and the cotton, farmers were forced to take out loans to buy the seed, and a spiral of debt and famine brought India to extreme poverty, a cycle that brought immense wealth to the Raj, but none to the people of India.

By spinning, by performing bread labor, the people helped break that cycle, and a nation awoke.

But in South Africa, where Gandhi first began his public work, bread labor was not spinning cotton. It was printing. It was typesetting. Printing was about spinning words into knowledge. At the Phoenix Ashram, everybody worked the printing press. Typesetting was their bread labor.

The printing press was a means to propagate knowledge, the means by which individuals educated themselves—and each other—the means by which they became a people, a people united, a people that won their satyagraha campaign. Knowledge gave birth to truth, and truth gave birth to freedom.

The increase and diffusion of knowledge is what we are doing here at Gandhi Bhavana, and I thank this amazing institution for giving us this beautiful home from which we can scan. We call ourselves the Servants of Knowledge. We are now digitising over 14 lakh pages every month. We hope to double that capacity soon.

Most of us involved in this endeavour have been practicing access to knowledge for many years. Our current efforts in Bengaluru began at the Indian Academy of Sciences, which gave us our first home. We used that base to digitise their materials, as well as many science books from CSRI laboratories.

We've continued those efforts in Mangaluru, where we helped put 4,000 books in Konkani online. We also assisted the Rojah Muthiah Library in Chennai, where we continue to work with a number of volunteers who are passionate about the Tamil language. Likewise, we work with Sanskrit and Telugu scholars who help improve the metadata of some of our online collections on the Internet Archive, a collection of over 8 lakh books in over 150 languages.

Here in Bengaluru, much of the credit for our work goes to my friend and colleague Omshivaprakash, who has been instrumental in putting thousands of books in Kannada online. His work goes back many years. He has assisted the Wikipedia and many other organizations, and has done seminal work that goes beyond mere digitisation, producing high quality dictionaries, fonts for the Kannada language, and so much more.

He's worked with publishers to make some of their older books available under a Creative Commons license so they may be freely used for noncommercial purposes. His work has been widely recognized throughout Karnataka, and I'm proud to work with him.

I'd also like to recognize two of my other colleagues who are with us here today.

Dr. Lawrence Liang is the founding dean of the School of Law at Ambedkar University Delhi, a winner of the prestigious Infosys prize, and a leading light in the fields of intellectual property and film studies.

Dr. Sushant Sinha is also here today. He is the creator of the amazing Indian Kanoon system that gives free access, not only to the legal profession but to all the people of India, to the judgements of the courts, the acts of legislatures, the official gazettes, and much more.

Both Lawrence and Sushant play an integral role in our efforts, and it is a great pleasure to work with them both.

Our scanning has been in many locations. Recently, we've worked with BMShri Prathistana, digitising large portions of their collections. For the last year we've been at the National Law School of India University, where we've digitised their entire library and will be making all those books available to the visually impaired at law schools across all of India.

Now we are here at Gandhi Bhavana. We are up and running and beginning to scan the entire library. We're very excited to be here.

GANDHI JAYANTI

Our efforts are focused on the public domain, and making knowledge available to all. The idea that the great riches in our libraries should be available to all also has deep roots in the philosophy of Gandhi-ji. When he was in London, there were three books that opened his eyes and changed his life.

The first, of course, was the Bhagavad Gita, which he read first in the English translation, the Song Celestial from Edwin Arnold. The text became a guiding light for him, as it is for many of you here today.

The second book was the Bible, which he learned about from an anonymous vegetarian from Manchester he met in a hotel, in particular the New Testament and especially the Sermon on the Mount. His reinterpretation of the meaning of that Sermon had a great effect on many Christians, especially Martin Luther King.

The third book was more obscure, a legal treatise called Snell on Equity, a textbook for law students, which is what he was at the time. From Snell, Gandhi-ji learned about trusteeship, a legal concept that led him to the idea that great wealth does not actually belong to the rich, it is only held in trust and "belongs to the community and must be used for the welfare of the community."

This holds true for libraries as well, which are trustees of knowledge. They are rich in books, but they hold them in trust for us.

But this concept is even broader, for we live in a democracy. We as citizens are the titular landlords, the owners of our government, but the reality is that we only hold our democracy in trust for the benefit of future generations.

This trusteeship is a serious responsibility, one we must take on with enthusiasm and devotion. As it says here in Bengaluru on the walls of the Vidhana Soudha, "government work is God's work."

Public work, bread labor, and trusteeship are three ideas that guide our own work. But, these concepts should be relevant to everybody.

For public work, for bread labor, we must each conduct our own experiments with truth, to contribute to our communities however we may. For us, that means scanning in order to promote the increase and diffusion of knowledge.

Perhaps you are in tech and you contribute to open source software, or you adopt and support your local nonprofit, or you contribute articles to the Wikipedia, or translate it into your language. The efforts can be big or they can be small. Maybe you tutor neighborhood children, or maybe you make two million school lunches a day like the Akshaya Patra Foundation here in Karnataka.

As Bob Dylan says, no matter what you do, no matter who you are, you've got to serve somebody.

You can contribute anyway you see fit. Bread labor is personal, it is the sweat of your brow. Public work is also personal, it is how you choose to be a citizen, how you choose to do your duty.

Do what you will, but do something. For the Servants of Knowledge, scanning is the new spinning. It is our bread labor, our public work.

Universal access to knowledge is the great promise of our times. Knowledge is the key that unlocks the doors to a better future.

Knowledge by itself is not enough. It must be combined with action. Dasimayya said that unless the fire joins the wind, it would not know how to move.

Bread labor and public work are the key to action. Knowledge is the wind, action is the fire. Knowledge is the key to how we educate ourselves, our children, our brethren, but it is more.

Knowledge is the key to opportunity.

Knowledge is the key to democracy.

Knowledge is the key to freedom.

Let us unlock those doors. Let us walk through them together.

Thank you coming today and thanks for inviting me. Happy Gandhi Jayanti to all of you. Thank you very much.

Democracy's Library
Internet Archive Hero Award
October 19, 2022

Thank you Corynne. Thank you Brewster. That was totally over the top, and I have to say how much I really appreciate that.

The three of us have spent so many years walking together up that crooked path. We are fellow travelers. I appreciate your company and your counsel and especially your friendship.

Good evening. My friends. Thank you for coming tonight.

Our verse for the day is "democracy's library." You've heard Brother Brewster preach his sermon earlier this evening. Let me just say amen to every single thing he said. He spoke truth.

Government information is more than just a good idea. It is about the law. It is about our rulebook. It is the manual on how we—we as citizens—how we choose to run our society. We own this manual.

Government information is the operating system of our society. It is the code by which we—we the people —by which we the people who own our democracies—

it is how we govern ourselves. These codes are law. These are edicts of government.

We are the trustees of our democracies. We are the board of directors. Every government official works for every one of us, and we must do our part to work for them. No one is coming, it is up to us.

But, we cannot be the trustees of our society today —we cannot honor our obligations for future generations—if we cannot freely read and speak and even change that rulebook.

Democracy's library is our foundational text. You have edit privileges. You have root. Use your superuser powers. But remember, with great power comes great responsibility.

John Adams famously said that a democracy cannot work without an informed citizenry. He was talking to you. He said we must "let every sluice of knowledge be set a-flowing" if we are to succeed as a fair and just and democratic society, a society that lifts us all up, because we are informed citizens. Because we can access and use and copy and speak from democracy's library.

But this library is for nothing if we do not use it to achieve that dream of a fair and just and democratic society that respects our peoples—all our peoples—

and respects our planet—and makes universal access to all knowledge a human right.

This is not an American idea. It is a global idea. It is not a north thing, not a south thing, it is not an east or west thing. It is a universal ideal.

It is a fundamental premise of the rule of law in any democracy that we know our rights and obligations. This is the principle of promulgation, a doctrine at the very heart of the rule of law.

My work is focused on America and India, the world's two largest democracies. But, the principle of promulgation is universal. Without democracy's library, you cannot have democracy, you do not have the rule of law.The library is essential. It is a bedrock. It is foundational. It is fundamental. This is our ground truth.

It is particularly apt that we are talking tonight about democracy's library at the Internet Archive, the Internet's public library, our town hall, our commons. I've had the privilege and the honor to work with the Internet Archive for the entire period it has existed, since 1996.

It is a sophisticated and powerful and amazing technical machine. For people like me who have been able to upload literally millions of government documents to this open repository—it has been my cloud.

The Internet Archive was where I was able to stash 14,000 hours of video of congressional hearings, it was where we put 20 years of IRS nonprofit returns, 6,000 videos copied from the National Archives, 19.8 million pages of PACER documents, over 25,000 legally mandated public safety standards, the legislative codes of a 14 US states, the jury instructions of 22 states, the regulations of all 50 states, not to mention 750,000 official gazettes from all the states of India and the Union Government, and Hind Swaraj, the definitive collection about India's fight for freedom.

I must thank—we really must all thank—everybody at the Internet Archive for the wonderful thing you have built and for the oh so competent and proficient and knowledgable and also, I must say, nice people who work at this amazing institution.

Tonight is special for me. I've always considered myself a civil servant who serves our government—and serves the people—despite not having an actual job, and it is so gratifying to have that recognized by you tonight.

While I accept this award with much gratitude, I have to turn it around. This is a communal effort. We are the government. We are the people. What can we do if we all work together? How can we pay this gift forward?

So, I thank you. For your praise, but also for the work all of you do, every day. We ar—all of us, we are the people that help build and run and improve the public side of our global Internet. Let us all take great pride in that tremendous accomplishment.

But this is also why we must try harder. We must work harder. We must seize this opportunity in front of us before we lose our moment in time.

This is our moment. We must seize the means of computation and make their fruits available to all the people. We must build a distributed and interoperable Internet for our global village. The increase and diffusion of knowledge must be our mutual mission. Let us all swim together in that ocean of knowledge.

Gandhi taught us that we must all be public workers, that we must all contribute to this global village—if we wish to make it a better place, to own our world—to fulfill our duties to each other as trustees. For Gandhi, he spun cloth and he blogged—he wrote prolifically, every day.

For us, scanning is the new spinning. Let us be the change we wish to see. We are the servants of knowledge.

In India, we say pVictory to Knowledge: Jai Gyan! Universal access to all human knowledge is the great promise of our time. Let us resolve tonight to keep that promise. We owe that to the future. They're counting on us.

Good night everybody. Have a wonderful rest of the evening, and thank you so much. This has been a real thrill. You've touched me deeply.

Thank you.

www.ingramcontent.com/pod-product-compliance
Lightning Source LLC
Chambersburg PA
CBHW050540210326
41520CB00012B/2650